NAUTICAL NONSENSE

Stephen Hillenburg

Based on the TV series *SpongeBob SquarePants*® created by
Stephen Hillenburg as seen on Nickelodeon®

ISBN 0-439-81737-4

12 11 10 9 8 7 6 5 4 3 2 1   6 7 8 9 10 11/0

Printed in the U.S.A.

First Scholastic printing, January 2006

NICK

SpongeBob SquarePants

Nautical Nonsense

A SpongeBob Joke Book

By Wendy Wax

SCHOLASTIC INC.

New York Toronto London Auckland Sydney
Mexico City New Delhi Hong Kong Buenos Aires

Why were SpongeBob's suspenders sent to jail?
For holding up his SquarePants.

What goes "Ha, ha, ha, plop!"?
SpongeBob laughing his head off.

What happened when SpongeBob sat on the chewing gum?
He became SpongeBob ChairPants.

Who is the snootiest sponge in Bikini Bottom?
SpongeSnob.

Why does SpongeBob prefer saltwater?
Because pepperwater makes him sneeze.

Where does SpongeBob point his sneeze?
Atchoo!

What did SpongeBob say to the Flying Dutchman?
How do you boo?

Who didn't clean his pineapple?
SpongeSlob.

SpongeBob: What doesn't get any wetter no matter how hard it rains?
Patrick: The ocean.

Why did Patrick bring a chocolate bar to his dentist appointment?
He wanted a chocolate filling.

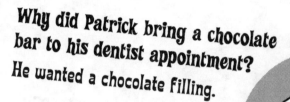

Why does Patrick prefer to swim at night?
He's a starfish.

Why did the bubble gum cross the road?
Because it was stuck to SpongeBob's shoe.

What was wrong with Patrick's pencil story?
It didn't have a point.

Why did Patrick walk as he played the guitar?
He wanted to get away from the noise.

What is the Flying Dutchman's favorite kind of party?
A come-as-you-were party.

Why did Squidward play his clarinet while standing on a chair?
So he could reach the high notes.

Why did Squidward keep his clarinet in the fridge?
So he could make cool music.

How does Squidward spell "disaster"?
S-P-O-N-G-E-B-O-B.

Squidward: Ouch! I threw out my back again.

SpongeBob: Check the trash before it's picked up!

Customer: Waiter! This coffee tastes like sand!

SpongeBob: That's because it was only ground this morning.

Knock-knock.

Who's there?

Dewey.

Dewey who?

Dewey have to eat Krabby Patties again?

What happened when the Flying Dutchman lost his anchor?

He haunted for it.

Why do some people call
Mr. Krabs a "doughnut"?
Because he loves money.

What is Mr. Krabs's favorite
part of the football game?
The quarterback.

How does Mr. Krabs double his money?
By folding it in half.

How much does Mr. Krabs eat?
Just a pinch.

What are two things Mr. Krabs refuses to serve for lunch?

Breakfast and dinner.

What happened when the Flying Dutchman got a job at the Krusty Krab?

He became the Frying Dutchman.

Why did Plankton stick a hose in Mr. Krabs's ear?
He was trying to brainwash him.

What did Larry the Lobster give the drowning lemons?
Lemon aid.

Where would you find Larry the Lobster on Halloween?
At the Boo Lagoon.

What does SpongeBob call Gary when he's riding in the passenger seat?

His carpet.

How did SpongeBob stop Gary from leaving slime in the backyard?
He put him in the front yard.

What did Pearl become on her trip to the Arctic?
A blue whale.

What musical did Mr. Krabs plan to take Pearl to see on her birthday?
Fiddler on the Reef.

NOW SHOWING...
Fiddler on the Reef

What did they do when the musical was sold out?
They saw a dive-in movie instead.

What did SpongeBob call Patrick
when he fell in the swamp?
Muddy buddy.

If Gary got in trouble, where would he go?
Snail jail.

How does Gary keep in touch with his family?

Snail mail.

Mrs. Puff: SpongeBob, have your eyes ever been checked?

SpongeBob: No, they've always been blue.

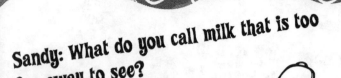

Sandy: What do you call milk that is too far away to see?

SpongeBob: Pasteurized.

Why did Mrs. Puff wear sunglasses to school? She had bright students.

Who did Mermaidman become when he got lost in the Arctic Ocean?
Brrr-maidman.

How much did Patchy the Pirate have to pay to get his ears pierced?
A buck an ear.

Who wears an eye patch and is always itchy?
Scratchy the Pirate.

How did SpongeBob make a jellyfishing net?
He sewed a bunch of holes together.

Patrick: What does a jellyfish have on its tummy?

SpongeBob: A jelly button.

SpongeBob: What is the best way to catch a jellyfish?

Patrick: Have someone throw it to you.

Patrick: What buzzes, wobbles, and flies?

SpongeBob: A jellycopter.

SpongeBob: What do you call a polar bear in Bikini Bottom?

Patrick: Lost.

Sandy: How does a boat show affection?
Patrick: It hugs the shore.

SpongeBob: What did one fish say to the other?
Squidward: If you keep your mouth closed, you won't get caught.

Books for Sale!

A Tourist's Guide to Bikini Bottom
by N. Joy Yerstay

Surfing Down Sand Mountain
by Howell I. Ever-Dewitt

The Krusty Krab Diet
by Watson Thimenue

Getting Rid of Plankton
by X. Terman Aite

Caring for a Pet Snail
by Walket Wunsaday

Sandy the Speedy Squirrel
by Sherwood Lyke Tewkatcher

How to Stop Procrastinating
by Alex Playne Layder

SpongeBob's Secret to Life
by M. Brace Itt

Mrs. Puff: What's the capitol of Bikini Bottom?

SpongeBob: The letter B.

SpongeBob: What do you call two pieces of seaweed that get married?

Sandy: Newlyweeds.

32

Mrs. Puff: What gallops through Bikini Bottom?

Patrick: A seahorse.

Knock-knock.
Who's there?
Doug.
Doug who?
Doug a hole in the sand.

What would you get if you cloned
SpongeBob five hundred times?
A SpongeMob!

Why didn't the judge believe the Flying Dutchman?
Because he could see right through him.

Who haunts underneath
SpongeBob's bed?
The Flying Dustman.

What is easy for SpongeBob and Patrick to get into but hard for them to get out of? Trouble.

How did SpongeBob make a bandstand?
He took away their chairs.

How did SpongeBob get straight As in Mrs. Puff's class?

He used a ruler.

What kind of steps did SpongeBob take when Squidward chased him out of the Krusty Krab?

Great big ones.

Why did Patrick install a knocker on his rock?
He wanted to win the No-Bell Prize.

When does the Flying Dutchman usually appear?
Just before someone screams.

Why was it windy at SpongeBob and Patrick's bubble-blowing show?
Because of all their fans.

Why did Patrick put a strawberry under his pillow?
He wanted to have sweet dreams.

Where in Bikini Bottom did Squidward see an annoyed cashier?

In the mirror.

Squidward: Where do fish go when they don't feel well?

SpongeBob: To a sturgeon.

SpongeBob: What do you call a fish with no eyes?

Patrick: A fsh.

Patrick: Do fish ever have holidays?

SpongeBob: No, they're always in schools.

SpongeBob: What smells like fries and is covered with lint?

Squidward: The Dusty Krab.

SpongeBob: What lives at the bottom of the sea and carries a lot of fish?

Mrs. Puff: An octobus.

Where is Patchy the Pirate's treasure chest?

Under his treasure shirt.

Mr. Krabs: Why did the fish tell excuses?

SpongeBob: To get off the hook.

What do you get when you cross Dracula with Patchy the Pirate?

A vampirate.

Why didn't SpongeBob do well on his report card?

Because his grades were below C-level.

How does SpongeBob know the sea is friendly?

It waves.

What game do Patrick and SpongeBob like to play?

Name That Tuna.

Mr. Krabs: Why did the fries run out of the restaurant?

Patrick: They were fast food.

What did SpongeBob break by saying its name? Silence.

Who is Squidward's favorite writer?
William Sharkspeare.

Why doesn't Plankton serve doughnuts?
He doesn't like the idea of the hole business.